ideals®
THANKSGIVING

The morns are meeker than they were;
    The nuts are getting brown.
The berry's cheek is plumper;
    The rose is out of town.

The maple wears a gayer scarf,
    The field a scarlet gown.
Lest I should be old-fashioned,
    I'll put a trinket on.

Emily Dickinson

ISBN 0-8249-1055-9

IDEALS—Vol. 44, No. 7 November MCMLXXXVII IDEALS (ISSN 0019-137X) is published eight times a year,
February, March, May, June, August, September, November, December
by IDEALS PUBLISHING CORPORATION, Nelson Place at Elm Hill Pike, Nashville, Tenn. 37214-8000
Second class postage paid at Nashville, Tennessee, and additional mailing offices.
Copyright © MCMLXXXVII by IDEALS PUBLISHING CORPORATION
POSTMASTER: Send address changes to Ideals, Post Office Box 148000, Nashville, Tenn. 37214-8000
All rights reserved. Title IDEALS registered U.S. Patent Office.
Published simultaneously in Canada.

SINGLE ISSUE—$3.95
ONE-YEAR SUBSCRIPTION—eight consecutive issues as published—$15.95
TWO-YEAR SUBSCRIPTION—sixteen consecutive issues as published—$27.95
Outside U.S.A., add $4.00 per subscription year for postage and handling.

Publisher, Patricia A. Pingry
Editor, Peggy Schaefer
Art Director, Lyman Black
Production Manager, Jan Johnson
Permissions, Kathleen Gilbert

Front and back covers from Freelance Photographers Guild

Inside front cover by Ed Cooper

Inside back cover from Freelance Photographers Guild

Autumn Morning

An autumn morning's fragile haze
Comes slipping through the trees
To touch the dawn-stilled waking world
With mellowness and ease.

It blends the myriad hues of fall
Into a patchwork lace
Of golds and reds and greens and browns
Across the landscape's face.

The sumac and the maple leaves,
A boarded country school,
Each has a new significance
When fall has come to rule.

Each song of brittle, dancing leaves,
Each flying goose's call,
Each caterpillar's silent march
Adds majesty to fall.

Craig E. Sathoff

Photo Opposite
MISTY MORN
Laatsch-Hupp Photo

Photo Overleaf
AUTUMN IN NEW YORK
E.J. Cyr
Cyr Color Photo

Home Again

Home again—it's good to be
Where the home lights softly glow,
'Midst the folks you love the best
And the many friends you know.
Mighty pleasant where the cheer
Of the fireside gleams, and then,
Flickers low to gleam once more—
Home again.

Home again—here one forgets
All the sorrows, all the care.
And it seems as though you dwell
In a world that's free from care.
Here is where those childhood days
Live again in memory when
You come back to stay awhile—
Home again.

Home again—how swift the years.
Steps sound heavy on the floor.
Age has changed so many folks
That you knew in days of yore.
But the laughter and the song
Bring once more the fleeting past.
How you revel in the wish
This experience might last—
Home again.

                              Howard Biggar

Photo Opposite
LINCOLN'S SPRINGFIELD HOUSE
Jeff Gnass

This Thanksgiving Day

Thankful may I ever be for everything that God bestows. Thankful for the joys and sorrows, for the blessings and the blows. Thankful for the wisdom gained through hardships and adversity. Thankful for the undertones as well as for the melody.

Thankful may I ever be for benefits both great and small—and never fail in gratitude for that divinest gift of all: the love of friends that I have known in times of failures and success. O may the first prayer of the day be always one of thankfulness.

Patience Strong

Photo Opposite
BRANT LAKE
Gene Ahrens

An Autumn Walk

Could this little old road be luring me now
Deep into autumn's fold;
Through the glorious light of the noonday sun
That illumines the trees of gold?

Through the vista that wanders and curves its way
Along the dreaming hill;
Through a radiant wood of leaves and boughs
That ring with the warblers' trill?

Could this little old road be enticing me now
Through the Indian summer heat,
Where the meadows are sprawling with flowers and grass,
And the orchard is mellow-sweet?

Where the faraway hill stirs and glistens anew
In the beautiful autumn glow?
Could this little old road be beckoning now—
My heart is eager and I must go!

Joy Belle Burgess

Photo Opposite
AUTUMN WALK
Appel Color Photography

Thanksgiving Time

The almond tree which gave its fruit
Is turning gold this fall.
The sumac in the colored wood
Has spread a flaming ball.
A farmer, grateful for the yield,
Sings out his harvest call.
Bright autumn is Thanksgiving time
When everything gives all.

Harold A. Schulz
Prattville, AL

Family Blessings

Heartwarming is the evening meal
With each one in his place;
When touched hands form a loving ring,
And heads bow to say grace.

When appetites are quickened by
The smell of still-warm bread,
And on the stove fat chestnuts roast,
And apples, green and red.

When Father looks at Mother with
A smile and tender love;
Ah! Then it is a family knows
God's blessings from above.

Martha Corrine Love
Greensburg, PA

Winter Warmth

The frost has turned corn stalks to brown.
Autumn's chill we've felt.
'Tis time to thank the one on high
For blessings we've been dealt.

The turkey, pumpkin, nuts, and fruits
Weigh down our humble board.
We gather near with all our friends
To thank our dearest Lord.

We pray; we eat; we laugh; we love:
This day's for hearts to keep.
It leaves a glow to warm the earth
All through her winter's sleep.

Patricia J. Yovonovitz
Tuscon, AZ

Reflections

Five Senses

For sight of friends and family,
For butterfly and bumblebee,
For every sunset that I see,
   I thank thee, Lord.

For taste of fruit, both tart and sweet,
For hearty meal and snacktime treat,
For every morsel that I eat,
   I thank thee, Lord.

For hearing voices soft or shrill,
For plaintive cry of whippoorwill,
For whistling train and whirring mill,
   I thank thee, Lord.

For touch of surface, smooth or rough,
For baby skin and leather tough,
For scaly bark and furry muff,
   I thank thee, Lord.

For smell of food I'm glad today,
For burning leaves and new-mown hay,
For fragrance of a rose bouquet,
   I thank thee, Lord.

Vivian Hansbrough
Columbia, MO

Thanksgiving

I offer to thee thanksgiving
For gentle summer rain
That falls like a benediction
On growing fields of grain,

For thy glory in the sunset,
Thy voice in the evening breeze,
Thy peace in the shades of twilight,
Thy beauty in flowers and trees.

I offer to thee thanksgiving,
Oh, grant me length of days
That through all the shining hours
My heart may sing thy praise.

Mary Fink
Zell, S.D.

Editor's Note: Readers are invited to submit unpublished, original poetry, short anecdotes, and humorous reflections on life for possible publication in future I*deals* issues. Please send copies only; manuscripts will not be returned. Writers will receive $10 for each published submission. Send materials to "Readers' Reflections," Ideals Publishing Corporation, Nelson Place at Elm Hill Pike, Nashville, Tennessee 37214.

Thanksgiving Day at Grandpa's

Thanksgiving Day at Grandpa's
Is the best day of the year;
It's filled to overflowing
With folks and fun and cheer.

The table's filled with good things
That stretch from wall to wall.
Grandma says there's always room
For loved ones, big or small.

I can smell the turkey roasting,
And I've seen the pumpkin pies.
Oh, it's so much harder waiting
With the food before your eyes!

Then just before we all sit down,
We bow our heads in prayer;
And Grandpa thanks our Father
For his blessings and his care.

That's really why we've gathered here—
Not just for food and play—
But to thank our Father for his gifts
On this Thanksgiving Day!

Joyce Butler Miller

Temptations

Just smell the turkey roasting;
The kids can hardly wait.
Delicious foods are cooking,
Pies heaped upon the plate.

Cranberries, red and juicy,
Rich dressing, golden-brown,
Potatoes served with gravy,
Fruit salads in a mound.

Jars are filled with cookies;
Tall cakes are iced in white.
The candy's done and cooling;
Let's try to sneak a bite.

The sounds of fun and laughter
Fill our home this holiday.
We feast on nature's bounty
In a tempting, bright array.

Cousins, aunts, and uncles
Are gathered by the score
To celebrate Thanksgiving;
Now who could ask for more?

Elisabeth Weaver Winstead

The Blessings of Home...

The street that fronted grass-edged walks
Before our childhood home
Pursued gay, crimson hollyhocks
Beneath a spangled dome.

It welcomed us when we recessed
To points away from hearth,
Away from walls that calmed, caressed,
Away from comfort's worth.

It welcomed us when we returned
With glowing tales to share
Of many things that we discerned
In God's peace-loving care.

Thus of the streets that brought applause
And rang beneath our feet,
It was our favorite because
It led to home's retreat.

Lydia O. Jackson

Dear Lord, may blessings of our home
Be shared with one and all;
The love and peacefulness we feel,
Enclosed within each wall.

May every guest who steps inside
Feel welcome, warm, sincere,
And know that we can share with them
This realm that we hold dear.

Lord, may we never turn away
A stranger from our door,
But cheerfully give him refuge and
The peace he's looking for.

May all the joy and peace we feel
Within this house we own,
Be shared with others who step in,
Not kept for us alone.

Carice Williams

Thanksgiving Postcards

Thanksgiving smiles in wine
  and yellow
A peaceful blessing on our lives.
The apples redden, pumpkins
  mellow;
The cornucopia arrives.

Potatoes bake with pie-sweet
  crusting;
Brown turkeys fill the glowing
  stoves.
Such bounty is the harvest-
  trusting
As kitchens smell of warm rich
  loaves.

The roads rerhyme a glad
  Thanksgiving
Through scarlet hills and
  goldenrod.
Hear now the song of freedom
  living;
View now the white prayer house
  of God.

Inez Franck

CRAFTSBURY COMMON, VERMONT
Appel Color Photography

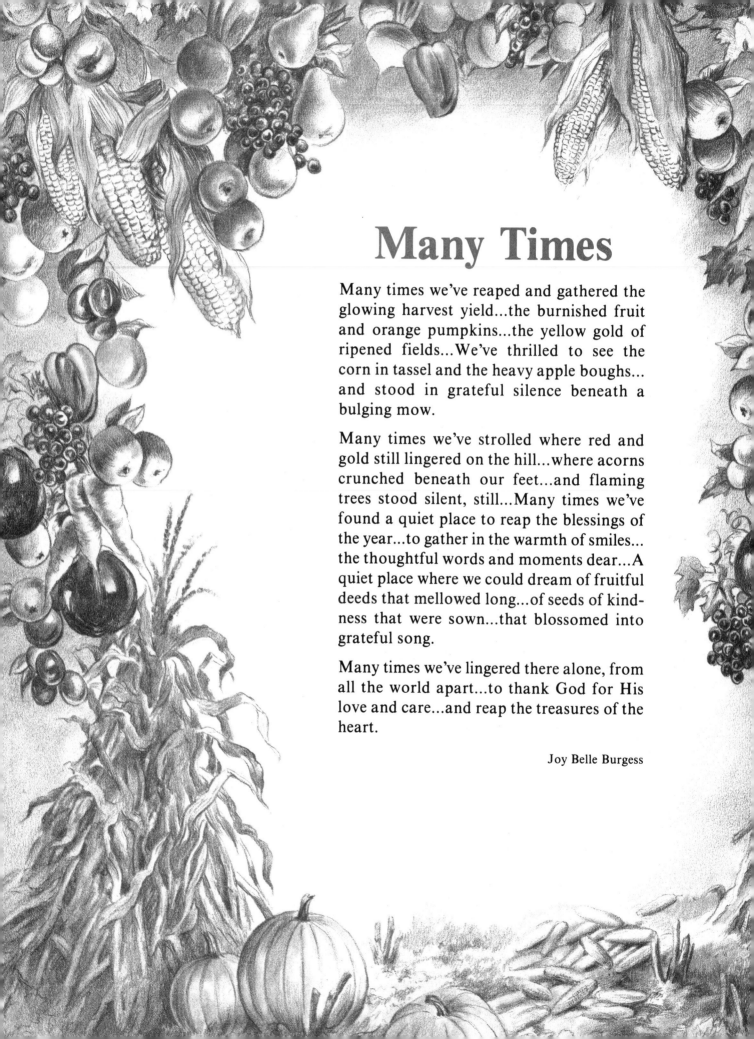

Many Times

Many times we've reaped and gathered the glowing harvest yield...the burnished fruit and orange pumpkins...the yellow gold of ripened fields...We've thrilled to see the corn in tassel and the heavy apple boughs... and stood in grateful silence beneath a bulging mow.

Many times we've strolled where red and gold still lingered on the hill...where acorns crunched beneath our feet...and flaming trees stood silent, still...Many times we've found a quiet place to reap the blessings of the year...to gather in the warmth of smiles... the thoughtful words and moments dear...A quiet place where we could dream of fruitful deeds that mellowed long...of seeds of kindness that were sown...that blossomed into grateful song.

Many times we've lingered there alone, from all the world apart...to thank God for His love and care...and reap the treasures of the heart.

Joy Belle Burgess

Hope and Harvest

O God of hope and harvest,
Who gives our daily bread,
Again at this Thanksgiving
We bow a grateful head.
Though corn and grain is gathered
In quite a different way,
We echo with our heartbeats
That first Thanksgiving Day.

We thank thee, God, for planting
That little pilgrim band,
And testing it with hardship
In this untested land;
For sowing with those seedlings
Ideals both strong and just
That caused an infant nation
To breathe, "In God we trust."

We thank thee, God, for giving
The fruits of faith again,
From fields of love and tillage,
From trust in thee and men.
Oh, God of hope and harvest,
Hear us who humbly pray
And thank thee for thy blessing
On this Thanksgiving Day.

Margaret Rorke

Selection

Heap high the farmer's wintry hoard!
 Heap high the golden corn!
No richer gift has autumn poured
 From out her lavish horn.

Let other lands exulting glean
 The apple from the pine,
The orange from its glossy green,
 The cluster from the vine.

But let the good old corn adorn
 The hills our fathers trod;
Still let us, for his golden corn,
 Send up our thanks to God.

John Greenleaf Whittier

Photo Opposite
ROADSIDE MARKET
Larry Lefever
Grant Heilman Photography

Abundance

Jellies sparkling row by row
On the basement shelves below,
Apples pouring from their bins
Say Thanksgiving's here again.

Golden pumpkins in their place,
Jars of mincemeat clearly state,
What a happy feast there'll be,
This Thanksgiving Day, you see.

Crispy pickles, steaming pies
With the frosting piled up high,
Crunchy cakes and puddings, too,
Made especially for you.

The turkey's browning—Oh! so nice;
The ham is done and set aside;
Grateful hearts now humbly wait
For each one to take his place.

Hearts that overflow with praise
On this day, of all days,
Set aside to honor thee
For country, home, and liberty.

Louise Forester Pryor

Thanksgiving Mincemeats

Mincemeat

- 1 pound beef
- ½ pound suet
- 4 pounds apples
- ½ pound currants
- 1 pound raisins
- 1½ pounds brown sugar
- 1 quart cider
- 1 cup meat stock
- 2 teaspoons salt
- 1 teaspoon cloves
- 1 teaspoon nutmeg
- 2 teaspoons cinnamon
- 5 tablespoons lemon juice

Grind beef and suet (or use 1½ pounds fatty ground beef). Pare, core, and chop apples. Chop together currants and raisins. Mix apples, currants, raisins, sugar, cider, and meat stock. Cook about 5 minutes. Add beef, suet, and seasonings to apple mixture. Simmer 1 hour, stirring frequently to keep from burning. Add lemon juice.

Green Tomato Mincemeat

- 5½ cups chopped green tomatoes
- 5½ cups chopped apples
- 8 cups brown sugar
- ½ teaspoon cloves
- 1 teaspoon nutmeg
- 1 teaspoon cinnamon
- 2 pounds chopped raisins
- 2 teaspoons salt
- 1 cup chopped suet *or* ground beef
- 1 cup vinegar
- 1 orange rind, grated

Chop tomatoes and drain thoroughly. Measure juice and add an equal amount of water to the pulp. Heat until scalding hot. Drain off liquid. Repeat two times: adding fresh water, scalding, and draining. Add the chopped apples to the tomatoes. Add sugar mixed with spices, raisins, salt, and suet. Cook until clear. Add remaining ingredients and cook until mixture thickens and flavors are blended. Pack into hot, sterilized jars and seal.

Photo Opposite, MINCEMEAT PIE, from
From Mama's Kitchen Cookbook, copyright © 1976 by
Catharine P. Smith, Published by Ideals Publishing Corporation.

Mince Pie with Oatmeal Crust

Crust

- ¾ cup flour
- ½ teaspoon salt
- ½ cup quick-cooking rolled oats
- ⅓ cup shortening
- 4 tablespoons cold water

Sift together flour and salt. Stir in rolled oats. Cut in shortening and sprinkle dough with cold water. Stir until just dampened. Roll out on floured board and fit into 9-inch pie pan.

Filling

- 2½ cups prepared mincemeat
- ⅓ cup brown sugar
- 2 tablespoons flour
- ¾ cup whipping cream
- ½ cup chopped pecans

Pour mincemeat into unbaked pie shell. Combine brown sugar and flour. Add whipping cream and blend well. Pour cream mixture over mincemeat. Sprinkle with pecans. Bake at 425° for 15 minutes. Reduce heat to 325° and bake 15 to 20 minutes longer or until done.

Pumpkin-Mincemeat Pie

- 1 unbaked 9-inch pie shell
- 2 cups cooked pumpkin
- ¾ cup brown sugar
- ¾ teaspoon cinnamon
- ¼ teaspoon nutmeg
- ⅛ teaspoon ginger
- ⅛ teaspoon cloves
- ½ teaspoon salt
- 2 eggs, beaten
- 1 cup evaporated milk
- 1 cup mincemeat

Combine pumpkin, sugar, spices, and salt. Add beaten eggs and mix well. Gradually add evaporated milk, stirring until well blended. Set aside. Spread mincemeat over bottom of pie shell. Pour pumpkin mixture over mincemeat. Bake at 375° for 45 minutes or until a knife inserted into center of pie comes out clean. Cool. Garnish with whipped cream if desired.

Thanksgiving Time

Editor's Note for "Thanksgiving Time"

Laura wrote that "everything came at us out of the West...storms, blizzards, grasshoppers, burning hot winds, and fire...yet it seemed that we wanted nothing so much as we wanted to keep on going west." For her father, this urge to travel west was inherent. The Burr Oak life was too constraining for him, and after two years there, the Ingalls family returned to Walnut Grove.

The family lived in town, where Pa worked as a miller, operated a butcher shop, and did carpentry. But he was torn between wanderlust and responsibility. The burdens increased when Mary became ill with spinal meningitis and lost her eyesight in 1879. From then on, Laura assumed the role as Mary's link to color, light, and action, using her quick tongue and descriptive powers.

By 1879, the Chicago and Northwestern Railroad had reached Tracy, Minnesota, seven miles west of Walnut Grove. The company then extended its tracks into Dakota Territory. As the railroad was built, new towns sprang up along its tracks, and easterners were encouraged to claim the "free land" of the prairies. Charles Ingalls was anxious to claim a new homestead.

During the summer of 1879, Pa served as timekeeper and paymaster for the Big Sioux River camp near present-day Brookings, South Dakota, and then moved on to the Silver Lake camp near De Smet.

While Pa worked for wages and saved money, his family prepared to leave Walnut Grove. They were reunited at the Silver Lake camp, and Pa was satisfied with the rolling, treeless countryside. He promised his wife that this was journey's end; they would travel no more.

When the Silver Lake camp closed down for the winter, the railroad surveyor asked Pa Ingalls to remain in the abandoned camp to guard the company tools. The family would be allowed to live in the surveyor's house on the bank of Silver Lake, rent-free, with provisions to last until spring. They accepted the offer and settled into the comfortable house. And on one of his walks across the prairie, Pa found the homestead he wanted near De Smet.

The Ingalls family lived cozily in the surveyor's house during their first winter in Dakota Territory. They were miles from any neighbor, but they celebrated the holidays happily.

On November 20, 1916, thirty-seven years after that holiday season in Dakota Territory, Laura Ingalls Wilder shared these reflections on Thanksgiving with her *Missouri Ruralist* readers.

William Anderson

As Thanksgiving Day draws near again, I am reminded of an occurrence of my childhood. To tell the truth, it is a yearly habit of mine to think of it about this time and to smile at it once more.

We were living on the frontier in South Dakota then. There's no more frontier within the boundaries of the United States—more's the pity—but then we were ahead of the railroad in a new unsettled country. Our nearest and only neighbor was 12 miles away, and the store was 40 miles distant.

Father had laid in a supply of provisions for the winter and among them were salt meats, but for fresh meat we depended on Father's gun and the antelope that fed in herds across the prairie. So we were quite excited one day near Thanksgiving when Father hurried into the house for his gun and then away again to try for a shot at a belated flock of wild geese hurrying south.

We would have roast goose for Thanksgiving dinner! "Roast goose and dressing seasoned with sage," said sister Mary.

"No, not sage! I don't like sage and we won't have it in the dressing!" I exclaimed. Then we quarreled, sister Mary and I, she insisting that there should be sage in the dressing and I declaring there should not be sage in the dressing, until Father returned—without the goose! I remember saying in a meek voice to sister Mary, "I wish I had let you have the sage," and to this day, when I think of it I feel again just as I felt then and realize how thankful I would have been for roast goose and dressing with sage seasoning—with or without any seasoning—I could even have gotten along without the dressing. Just plain goose roasted would have been plenty good enough.

This little happening has helped me to be properly thankful even tho' at times the seasoning of my blessings has not been just such as I would have chosen.

Laura Ingalls Wilder

Praise ye the Lord. I will praise the Lord with my whole heart, in the assembly of the upright, and in the congregation.

The works of the Lord are great, sought out of all them that have pleasure therein.

His work is honourable and glorious: and his righteousness endureth for ever.

He hath made his wonderful works to be remembered: the Lord is gracious and full of compassion.

He hath given meat unto them that fear him: he will ever be mindful of his covenant.

He hath shewed his people the power of his works, that he may give them the heritage of the heathen.

The works of his hands are verity and judgment; all his commandments are sure.

They stand fast for ever and ever, and are done in truth and uprightness.

He sent redemption unto his people: he hath commanded his covenant for ever: holy and reverend is his name.

The fear of the Lord is the beginning of wisdom: a good understanding have all they that do his commandments: his praise endureth for ever.

Psalm 111

Photo Opposite
HARVEST HYMN
Gerald Koser

Five Kernels of Corn

April, 1622

'Twas the year of the famine in Plymouth of old;
The ice and the snow from the thatched roofs had rolled.
Through the warm purple skies steered the geese o'er the seas,
And the woodpeckers tapped in the clocks of the trees.
And the boughs on the slopes to the south winds lay bare,
And dreaming of summer, the buds swelled in the air.
The pale Pilgrims welcomed each reddening morn;
There were left but for rations five kernels of corn.
     Five kernels of corn!
     Five kernels of corn!
But to Bradford a feast were five kernels of corn!

"Five kernels of corn! Five kernels of corn!
Ye people, be glad for five kernels of corn!"
So Bradford cried out on bleak Burial Hill,
And the thin women stood in their doors, white and still.
"Lo, the harbor of Plymouth rolls bright in the spring,
The maples grow red, and the wood robins sing,
The west wind is blowing, and fading the snow,
And the pleasant pines sing, and arbutuses blow.
     Five kernels of corn!
     Five kernels of corn!
To each one be given five kernels of corn!"

O Bradford of Austerfield, haste on thy way.
The west winds are blowing o'er Provincetown Bay,
The white avens bloom, but the pine domes are chill,
And new graves have furrowed Precisioners' Hill!
"Give thanks, all ye people, the warm skies have come,
The hilltops are sunny, and green grows the holm,
And the trumpets of winds, and the white March is gone,
And ye still have left you five kernels of corn.
        Five kernels of corn!
        Five kernels of corn!
Ye have for Thanksgiving five kernels of corn!

"The raven's gift eat and be humble and pray,
A new light is breaking, and truth leads your way;
One taper a thousand shall kindle: rejoice
That to you has been given the wilderness voice!"
O Bradford of Austerfield, daring the wave,
And safe through the sounding blasts leading the brave,
Of deeds such as thine was the free nation born,
And the festal world sings the "Five kernels of corn."
        Five kernels of corn!
        Five kernels of corn!
The nation gives thanks for five kernels of corn!
To the Thanksgiving feast bring five kernels of corn!

Hezekiah Butterworth

Our Forefathers

God watched and gave the Pilgrims strength;
He walked with them each day.
When weariness beset the tasks,
His hand with comfort lay.

Through fear and poverty they trod
For freedom's way to see,
With faith beyond understanding
To bring them liberty.

Despite the Pilgrim's years of hardship,
Their courage won a place,
Written in blood through history
For all the human race.

Olive Dunkelberger

Thanksgiving Legacy

The snow fell fast, the forest trees,
   Their heavy branches lowered,
And wildly raged the bitter wind,
   And loud the ocean roared.

Half buried in the drifted snow,
   The town of Plymouth stood—
Before, the tossing ocean lay,
   Behind, the wintry wood.

The homes were made of rough-hewn logs;
   The rude block-house stood near,
But from it rang the village bell
   In accents loud and clear.

And quickly people gathered there—
   Men, ladies, maidens gay—
To keep with gratitude sincere
   The first Thanksgiving Day.

And now a mighty nation stands,
   Its gratitude to pay,
To pray, besides, for strength and peace
   On this Thanksgiving Day.

Gary Radcliffe

Legacy

The angry ocean turned toward shore
   A darkly scowling face;
The forest stretched its threatening arms
   About the clearing place.

There Pilgrims humbly knelt to thank
   The God they prayed would bless
Their dream of faith, the hope they brought
   Into this wilderness.

That dream became reality;
   We fling its emblem high
In blazing stripes and spangled stars
   Beneath a clean, free sky.

The loom of God wove freedom's flag—
   An everlasting proof
Of living faith that forms the warp
   And hope that makes the woof.

Thanksgiving lives from year to year,
   Through every passing day,
Where man can kneel to praise his God,
   Each in his own free way.

Vivian Reeves

Pilgrim Fathers

Pilgrim Fathers, stern but true,
Our hearts give thanks today for you!
No fear didst lurk within thy breasts,
No flinching from life's trying tests!

God-fearing pioneers, you came
To found a country in his name,
That freedom's fires might always burn
And cowardice thy children spurn!

On a bleak and barren shore,
With frigid blast and scanty store,
'Midst imperiled, death-thinned ranks,
Thou didst proclaim a day of thanks!

Pilgrim Fathers, stern but true,
Our land again needs men like you!
Men who are gripped by but one fear—
Failure to preserve thy gifts so dear!

We, thy descendants, on this day
Salute thy courage as we pray!
May thy spirit tread our land again,
And God be honored now as then!

Elva Gladys Knox

The Lost Colony

In 1584, years before the Pilgrims came to America, Sir Walter Raleigh received a patent from Elizabeth I, Queen of England, to establish the first English settlement in the New World.

Raleigh, an English courtier and poet, immediately sent two men to explore the North American coast and bring back reports of its riches. The explorers returned with tales of a vast fertile land with rolling hills, tall trees, and an abundance of game. Encouraged by these reports, Raleigh started a colony in the new land, which he named Virginia.

He arranged for a small group of men to settle on the northern end of Roanoke Island near the coast of what is today North Carolina. For protection against unknown enemies, the colonists built a fort—which they named Fort Raleigh—and constructed houses around it.

When supplies ran low, the governor of the colony returned to England for help and left the colonists to explore their new home. Many of them grew homesick and some were disappointed to find no gold or other riches in the New World. They were not accustomed to the fertile soil of the area and planted few, if any, useful crops. When Sir Francis Drake, an English navigator, stopped at Roanoke during his explorations, the frustrated colonists boarded his ships and sailed back to England.

A few months later, the governor of Virginia returned to the new land with more supplies and was surprised to find the area deserted. He left fifteen members of the ship's crew to wait for the arrival of more settlers.

In 1587, Raleigh appointed John White the new governor of Roanoke. White and 150 other men, women, and children sailed across the Atlantic Ocean to fortify the struggling colony, but when they arrived, there was no sign of the fifteen men left on the island. Only a skeleton remained as proof of the early colonists. The fort had been destroyed, and only a few of the houses were standing.

Despite this, the colonists settled in, and on August 18, 1587, a baby girl was born to Ananias and Elinore Dare. Mrs. Dare, who was Governor White's daughter, named her baby Virginia after the new land. Virginia Dare was the first English child born in the New World.

Nine days after the birth of his granddaughter, Governor White returned to England for supplies. The colonists agreed that if they had to leave the colony, they would scratch the sign of a cross in a tree as a distress signal.

When Governor White reached England, he was told he could not return to Roanoke because all the large ships England had were being used in the war against Spain. Two smaller ships were sent to the island, but they never reached Roanoke. No other help was sent to the colonists.

In 1591, Governor White returned to the island, but found no one. He saw that the settlers had torn down their houses and rebuilt them inside a row of tall pointed logs. Near the entrance of the structure, someone had peeled the bark off a tree and on the smooth wood, had carved the word "Croatoan." But there was no sign of a cross.

Governor White thought the colonists had moved to nearby Croatoan Island or gone to live with friendly Croatoan Indians. But they were never found. The governor returned to England without knowing the fate of his granddaughter or any of the other settlers.

Modern scholars believe the colony was destroyed by Indians or that the colonists settled with a friendly Indian tribe, but no proof remains of what actually happened.

Heartbeat

From Valley Forge to Disneyland,
    there beats a heart of gold
Across this hallowed rock and sand,
    where legends still unfold.
Our flag still stands for freedom,
    where humble people pray,
In the country and the cities
    across the U.S.A.

The spirit of the pioneer
    abides within this land,
Where refugees from far and near
    receive a helping hand.
We're a nation bound together
    by a universal dream,
So we work and play together
    and form a mighty team.

From the mountains to the prairie,
    from coal mines to the sea,
The heartbeat of America
    is alive in you and me.
As spring turns into summer,
    and summer turns to fall,
There's a feeling of Thanksgiving;
    God bless us one and all!

Clay Harrison

BLUE RIDGE CABIN
Gene Ahrens

A Step into the Past

Each year, thousands of visitors from around the world step into the past at Plimoth Plantation and encounter a history lesson they will never forget.

Plimoth Plantation, the outdoor living history museum of 17th century Plymouth, re-creates a historical era through its major exhibits: the full-scale replica ship, *Mayflower II*, the 1627 Pilgrim Village, and a Wampanoag Indian Campsite.

Based on extensive research, museum curators and researchers have reconstructed the early colony as authentically as possible. The timber-frame houses, their furnishings, the kitchen gardens, the Wampanoag wetus, even the animals, appear as they probably did in 1627.

The most exciting re-creation is the people themselves. Staff called "interpreters" are trained to impersonate colonists and seamen who crossed the Atlantic in 1620, and those who came later to establish the first English colony in New England. Interpreters must absorb volumes of information on the period to develop a true mindset of the 17th century people they portray. They dress in period clothing, speak in the dialects of the era, and live the daily routine of the colonial farming community. As a result, visitors to the museum literally step into a time warp.

Aboard *Mayflower II*, visitors meet the likes of Master Christopher Jones, captain of the ship, and other crewmen and passengers who tell of their journey to the New World. Visitors are free to roam topside and between decks to see for themselves the cramped quarters where the 102 passengers lived during their historic 66-day voyage.

In the 1627 Pilgrim Village, staff portray known colonists such as Edward Winslow, Myles Standish, and John and Priscilla Alden. Their chores follow the seasonal cycle of the farming community: they plant in the spring, tend fields and gardens in the summer, harvest and preserve food in the fall. The harvest is the focus of all their labors, since their survival depends upon a successful harvest.

Visitors will see Pilgrim women cook meals

over the hearth, grind corn, sew, chop firewood, tend children and livestock, and bake breads and pies in the outdoor bake oven. Pilgrim men conduct militia drills, tend the fields, thatch roofs, hew beams, and rive clapboards. Men and women alike join in the raising of village houses.

Conversing with these folks from the past is the most engaging aspect of a visit to Plimoth Plantation. All are quick to explain why they came to this country, compare life here with life in England, describe their hopes for prosperity, or repeat some village gossip. But be warned—the conveyor of gossip could land in the stocks!

In the Wampanaog Summer Campsite, museum staff have constructed wetus, dome-shaped dwellings of bent saplings covered with woven reed mats. Visitors may sit on a bed covered with beaver pelts and savor an authentic native enviroment. Nearby are baskets, hemp bags filled with seeds, and a hoe made from the shoulder blade of a deer. A kettle rests above the cooking pit in the center of the dirt floor. An interpreter may tell tales describing the rich history and culture of the Wampanoag.

Each conversation aboard *Mayflower II,* in the Pilgrim Village, or Wampanoag Campsite is not idle chatter, but a conscious effort to impart knowledge of an earlier time to a diverse and contemporary public. The museum seeks to stir the mind and imagination of the visitor, to teach history, and to change stereotypical concepts of colonial life, about the Wampanoag or the Pilgrims. In the end, it is the visitor who becomes the interpreter of life as it was lived in colonial Plymouth.

Since everything in the Village, the Campsite, and the *Mayflower* is a reproduction, visitors are encouraged to handle tools, kitchen platters, beaver pelts, even try their hands at grinding corn, riving clapboards, fetching water, or chopping firewood.

Special events at all three sites heighten the visitor awareness of life in the early colony. Historically documented weddings and visits from the Dutch of New Amsterdam occur each year. Fur trading, general militia musters, court sessions, sailing of the *Mayflower's* shallop, even a visit from Massasoit give the visitor a sense of a living, working colony.

On Thanksgiving

I'm thankful for so many things
On this Thanksgiving Day;
My heart is filled with happiness
For blessings come my way—

The warmth and comfort of my home,
The love that I find there,
And all my golden memories
That shine with beauty rare.

I'm thankful for my loyal friends,
The laughter and the tears,
The dreams and hope and faith I have
To chase my doubts and fears;

For freedom in this land of ours,
The right to work and plan
To strive to reach the highest goal
And do the best I can.

But most of all I'm thankful for
The joy I find in prayer,
To let God know I'm grateful
For his constant love and care.

LaVerne P. Larson

Photo Opposite
SOUTH STRAFFORD, VERMONT
Fred Dole

For This Our Bounty

For this, our bounty, Lord, we give thee thanks
With grateful hearts as brimming as our store.
Our flocks are fed, our fields have yielded well,
Dear Lord, we could not rightly ask for more.
Pray, make us humble in our gratitude
And mindful of our brother's sore distress;
Unless in our abundance he may share
Then empty is our show of thankfulness.

We thank thee for this smiling land of ours,
For all the beauty and the grandeur here;
We thank thee most for freedom, dearly bought
By Pilgrim band and sturdy pioneer.
Had they not bravely fought, and so endured,
This priceless gift could never have been gained;
In thanks and solemn pride we raise the flag
And vow to keep its honor still unstained.

Marian F. Farrington

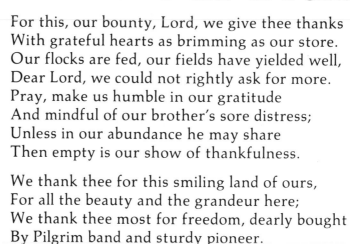

Goodness and Glory

Thanksgiving is my share of goodness
As autumn's harvest gifts abound;
The countryside reveals his blessing
Where pumpkins, corn, and nuts are found.
The bounty waits upon the table
While kinfolks gather lovingly;
My heart responds with grateful praising
And feels that He is good to me.

Thanksgiving is my share of glory
When nature wears a yellow crown:
The woods are like a golden temple
With orange and scarlet tumbling down.
Each road leads home to dreams and visions
Forefathers gave this freedom land;
Aware of faith and fruit and wonder,
I'm thankful for His generous hand.

Inez Franck

Photo Overleaf
OUR DAILY BREAD
Skip Schmiett
Royce Bair and Associates

Thanksgiving Is...

Turkey stuffed to overflowing and roasted
golden-brown;
Skaters on the old mill pond spreading laughter
all around;
Pumpkin pies and mincemeat pies spicing up the
air;
Children's laughter floating like a symphony
down the stair;

Chestnuts roasting on the hearth; the old folks
congregating
In a quiet corner by themselves, fond bygone
tales relating;
Heads bowed low in reverence to hear
Grandfather pray
And thank the Lord for such a spread on this
Thanksgiving Day.

Mrs. Paul E. King

Be Thankful!

When you wake up in the morning and watch the sun
   creep through
A dark and dismal flock of clouds that shaded it
   from view,
And you listen for the song of birds that heralds each
   new day,
Then be thankful for your blessings and bow your head
   to pray.

Just say a simple, "Thank you, God," for home and
   friends and neighbors,
But most of all say, "Thank you," for the blessings of
   your labors.
Be thankful for your country and the freedom of this
   land
That allows a man to pick or choose the lifestyle he has
   planned.

Be thankful for the freedom to worship as you please
And know that family, home, or wealth will never be
   besieged.
When the day has ended, and the sun sinks in the west,
Be thankful for a chance to say, "I've always had the
   best."

Margaret Bilbon

Little Thanksgivings

Thanksgiving leaves me overwhelmed with gratitude—gratitude to God for granting me another year, for giving me a home and health, for all the blessings he has provided so abundantly; gratitude to my country, for providing a place where I can live with the freedom to express my thanks as I wish; gratitude to my family for knowing all my faults and eccentricities, and accepting me just the same.

One Thanksgiving a few years ago, I came upon something that caused me to look at my favorite holiday from a slightly different perspective. Tucked between the pages of a favorite book, I discovered a slip of paper, yellowed with age. On it were scrawled a few lines of encouragement from an old friend. The note, sent at a time when I was deeply distressed, had been a ray of sunlight in my darkened life. I had read it over and over.

Simple as it was, the note had been a turning point in my life, lifting me out of depression. As I re-read it now, I couldn't recall ever thanking the writer.

Finding it just before Thanksgiving put the note in a new light. How many other seemingly small incidents in my life had passed without a thank-you? It was good, I thought, to be thankful to God, my country, and family; but wasn't it also important to be thankful to all the others in my life who had encouraged, praised, and helped me? Their input, tender and timely, had smoothed rough places, melted mountains, and bridged dark canyons of despair.

Intrigued by this idea, I sat at my desk and walked slowly through my memories, from childhood on, stopping here and there to jot down a name. There was a kind neighbor, Mrs. Cavanaugh, who shared my childish appreciation for a crisp dill pickle and always kept a jar in her refrigerator. I recalled

Mrs. Schindler, my third-grade teacher, who let me spend an entire afternoon coloring a lovely pink flamingo because she knew I was moving away and didn't want to go. That kindness meant so much to me then, but I'm sure Mrs. Schindler never knew. I smiled as I remembered my best friend in sixth grade, who had let me wear her favorite locket for a whole week. How elegant I had felt with that genuine gold-tone treasure dangling around my neck. What self-confidence it had produced! I thought of Mrs. Tapping, my ballet instructor, who recognized that my heart loved the dance, despite the contrary evidence from my unwilling limbs.

So many kindnesses, piled one upon the other, spilled over to influence my personality. I had never stopped before to analyze how much of myself had been formed by another's touch.

After an hour or so, my list was long with names of unthanked friends, acquaintances, and neighbors who had unwittingly contributed to the richness of my life. I had no idea where most of them were now and had no means of thanking them. They probably would even think it odd for me to thank them now for such a long-ago and simple kindness, but still, I felt like a banker with my accounts all out of balance.

I resolved that day to be more prompt in paying my debts of gratitude, and it led to a delightful discovery. That warm and wonderful feeling I get at Thanksgiving can be mine all year. Now I am more aware of small kindnesses and thoughtful words, and now, when I discover them, I offer thanks immediately.

A few words or a small note of appreciation takes so little time, and yet makes such a big difference in the quality of life. It becomes an endless circle of blessing and gives each day the opportunity to become a little Thanksgiving. Now I find I can enjoy my favorite holiday all year long!

Pamela Kennedy

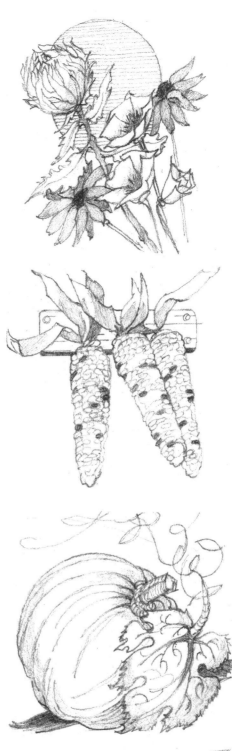

God's Been Good to Me

I'm mindful of the blessings
     that come my way each day.
My heart is overflowing
     each time I kneel to pray.

I'm thankful for the seasons;
     each one's a masterpiece.
I'm allowed to work the land,
     but God still holds the lease.

I'm grateful for the friendships
     that brighten sorrow's way,
Because my cup of happiness
     sustains me every day.

I love the children and the flowers
     that decorate my life
And the quiet, gentle hours
     I spend with my wife.

I'm grateful for eyes that see
     the beauty of it all
Because God's been good to me
     and blessed me through it all.

I'm thankful for the little things
     that fill my life with love.
The best things in life are free;
     they come from God above!

Clay Harrison

ADIRONDACK PARK, NEW YORK
Tom Algire

Country Chronicle

In November, when we are through with the land, newly plowed furrows flow like lyrical lines through fields of stubble and sod. The share of the plow seems to turn my thoughts and emotions into poetic passages written rhythmically across the pages of the land. I see the furrows as reminders of all that for which I should be thankful—they represent the end of a bountiful harvest and the sunset of a year's work.

I think back to my years as a hill farmer, in the time before the tractor replaced the team. For many autumns, I enjoyed following the horses as we plowed, watching the glistening furrows turned to the sun, listening to the creaking and straining of harness, the steel share against soil and stone, a cricket's chirp, a song sparrow's melody. I often witnessed huge flocks of wild geese in migration, flying high overhead in V-formations toward the warmer waters of the Gulf. I would stand in awe, listening to the clamor of their calls until they had flown beyond sight and sound and I returned to my task.

Stubble, the loose ground where corn was grown, was the first to be plowed because it was the first to freeze. On these hills, corn shocks stood like Indian tepees in the glorious October weather, serving as wigwams for the mouse until the corn was hauled to the barn.

The sod of the old meadows was the last to freeze and the last to feel the plow. The meadow, with its cover of grass and weeds, could hold the warmth of summer well into autumn. But by late November, it, too, had been plowed.

On Thanksgiving Day, I would look out over these plowed fields, their smooth and even furrows ready for snow, resting and waiting for spring and another seeding time. To me, the furrows were a sign of God's gifts and the wonder of nature. They still help me feel the kinship between man, nature, and the land. And on Thanksgiving, I bow my head in reverence to God and his providence; it is he who sustains my faith, my hopes, my dreams.

Lansing Christman

God's Gold

Oh, the glory of this autumn day,
When the trees unfold their gold!
Oh, how lifted is my spirit, Lord,
When such beauty I behold!

Like precious coins, each leaf holds on
Through sunshine, fog, or haze;
The memory of this rich display
Will warm my winter days.

Helen Kitchell Evans

Autumn's Glory

Today I saw such splendor
And heard the murmur of the trees
As I walked through autumn's glory,
Finding treasures in the leaves.

Through gold of elm and hackberry
And the firethorn's tawny shade,
While the maples added brilliance
Like bright banners on parade.

October brings fulfillment
To the promise of the spring.
Now the fields are ripe for harvest;
Indian summer reigns supreme.

All the land is paying tribute
To the summer's fruitful year;
It's the season of Thanksgiving
For autumn gifts garnered here.

Lela Meredith

Photo Opposite
MT. TIMPANOGOS, UTAH
Josef Muench

The Hearthside

When the autumn winds are blowing,
And there's frost upon the pane,
The snow drifts pile high
Over town and country lane.

Oh, then it is so pleasant
To sit by the hearthside stone,
As your loved ones gather round you,
Lovely hours are your own.

The red flames leap and crackle,
Giving warmth and special cheer;
The hearthside is a magic place
At this certain time of year.

It's easy for your mind to dream
While gazing at the glow,
And picture far off places
Or memories of long ago.

Comfortable and cozy,
The hearthside makes a home,
Where it's good to be in autumn
While the sky's a snow-filled dome.

It draws a family closer
And shines with love and cheer;
The hearthside is the heart of home
When autumn days and nights are here.

LaVerne P. Larson

Photo Overleaf
PLYMOUTH, VERMONT
Fred Dole

Flaming Hills

Maple fingers of flaming red
Reach out and touch the golden crown
Of aspen leaves now bending,
While autumn winds blow down.

While oak is dressed in her carmine frock,
She stands so stately and so strong.
Her leaves still cling while cold winds blow;
They'll hold on tight till winter's gone.

The grasses that were once so green
Have turned to many shades of brown;
And weeds, their pods have opened up
To let their tender seeds spill down.

As the clouds seem lower and so gray
And the days grow colder still,
I find myself wrapped up in fall
Amid the flaming hills.

Dorothy Behringer

Song of Autumn

Let us sing a song of autumn,
Of the apples sweet and mellow,
Of the sumac on the hillside
And the goldenrod so yellow.

Let us sing now of the stillness
And the fir trees faintly sighing,
Of the woodlands gently stirring,
Mourning for the birds gone flying.

Let us sing a song of autumn
As the painted leaves go winging,
For it is a glorious season—
Beauty, peace, and quiet bringing.

Johanna Terwee

Autumn Snowfall

I have seen many sights in my life
Which took my breath away, but I know
That never have I seen one like this—
The autumn scene overlaid with snow.

Oh, I could hardly believe my eyes
When the soft white flakes began to fall
On golden maples and crimson oaks
Which soon magically covered all.

Through their sudden frosting, chrysanthemums
Still glow in bronze and yellow and red;
And against the pewter of the sky,
Each pumpkin wears a white cap on its head.

The old rail fence is topped with icing,
Just like spice cake; and dark green hemlocks,
In counterpoint amid painted trees,
Are parading in new ermine smocks.

Truly a scene of real enchantment
Is this breathtaking autumn snowfall,
One that only the Master Designer
Could stage, enriching the hearts of all.

Earle J. Grant

When Autumn Slips to Winter

When autumn slips to winter on a cool November morn
And the frost is sparkling brightly, on the shocks of golden corn,
The world a lovely picture, as the darkness turns to light
The leaves fall thick and heavy, in a turbulent delight.

When winter comes so softly as the autumn hurries by
And we see a cloud of flurries, in the once so sunny sky,
With the wind a little sharper, and the grass not quite as green
The outdoors brightly different, in the changing autumn scene.

When autumn's nearly over, and the trees are all but bare
When the friendly clouds hang heavy, in the cool November air,
It's a melancholy feeling, as we realize once more
That the winter is approaching, right outside our autumn door.

When autumn sighs and whispers, as her stay is almost through
And a bit of old man winter, sneaks into her sky of blue,
It's a thrill beyond all measure, as we note the changing scene,
When autumn slips to winter, in a pleasant glowing dream.

Garnett Ann Schultz

November

The pasture stones are rimmed with frost;
The once-filled pond is dry.
Blueberry bushes flaunt red flags
Beside the winter rye.

The munching cows prolong their day;
The cornstalks, golden, stand.
The silo's fill with juicy feed
As neighbors lend a hand.

The crows are silent on the hill;
The beavers race the day.
The barns along the valley roads
Bulge with fragrant hay.

At midnight, when the wind is high,
A million stars are hung
Among the naked branches
Where summer birds have sung.

The lanes are carpeted with gold;
The rolling hills glow red.
November has its beauty, too,
When brighter days have fled!

Dorothy E. Begg

Winter's on the Way!

The nip is in the air again,
  And winter's on the way.
See how the trees stand leafless now
  And tiny snowflakes stray?

The month is late November, and
  Thanksgiving Day is here,
With Christmas Day to follow
  And finish out the year.

I love this gladsome time of year
  When holidays draw nigh,
When everyone is happy, and
  Spirits soar on high!

So snuggle by the fireside
  This sharp and windy day;
The nip is in the air again,
  And winter's on the way!

                        Georgia B. Adams

The Edge of Winter

We're on the edge of winter now;
  Snow flurries fill the air.
Look to the hills; see how the trees
  Stand destitute and bare.

The few stray leaves left from the fall
  Are tossing aimlessly;
The slate-gray sky looks ominous,
  And winds are blowing free.

We're on the edge of winter now;
  I see signs everywhere.
Come, take a long brisk walk with me,
  While flurries fill the air!

                        Georgia B. Adams

Photo Opposite
SNOW-COVERED BRIDGE
Doug Emerson

Nature's Picture Book

Nature turns another page,
And there before our eyes,
Are leafless trees like winding roads
Mapped out against the skies.

How quickly she did leaf her way
Through summer's color bright.
She left behind a glimpse of green,
Then turned it out of sight.

The wind-torn pages fly on by;
And soon it is November.
The warmth of June's long summer days
Can only be remembered.

Now families gather round in prayer,
Give thanks and ask the blessing.
Thanksgiving Day has come again;
Another season's passing.

Then angels turn on Christmas stars,
And snow shines 'neath the light.
The world looks like a page untouched,
A sheet of purest white.

Elveria Blust

Snow on the Hill

Come, walk with me to the tall, broad hill
Which is now knee-deep in snow,
And see the white immaculate spread
That lies silently far below.

The bright sun casts a shimmering gleam
On the blanket so soft and white;
It decks the earth with a magic cloak
Which silently fell in the night.

The great trees stand tall and bare,
As if the land were deep in sleep,
Outlining beauty far and near
For the world of man to reap.

The snow-white blanket lies regally
Around each plant, white and serene;
The hills and rocks are hidden,
As if tucked beneath a dainty screen.

Standing upon the hill in awe and wonder,
Drinking of the beauty given free,
A miracle sent down from heaven
To nature lovers such as we.

Mamie Ozburn Odum

Begin a Holiday Tradition with *Ideals*

The next issue of *Ideals* will feature the spirit and tradition of Christmas. Carefully selected poetry and prose, together with breathtaking photography and art reproductions, will bring to you the joy of the holiday season.

At *Ideals,* we especially enjoy the Christmas issue and our readers who have shared it with us over the years. One reader, Aleene Redman of Hartford, Illinois, wrote to us about how *Ideals* has become a Christmas tradition in her family.

> *I'm one of your biggest fans. I have enjoyed your magazine for many years.*
>
> *My children, when they were small, would buy me special Christmas issues. It was something they could afford and it was something they were sure I would enjoy.*
>
> *I still have the old magazines and read them over and am reminded each time of the children's eager and happy faces.*
>
> *Last Christmas, one of my grandchildren presented me with a copy of* Ideals*. I'm sure his dad helped him pick it out—knowing how pleased I would be.*
>
> *Thank you again. I'm looking forward to my* Ideals*.*

Thank you, Mrs. Redman, for your kind words and the reminder that *Ideals* can be a beautiful and inspirational Christmas gift.

We hope all of our readers have a merry holiday season and enjoy the coming Christmas issue of *Ideals.*

ACKNOWLEDGMENTS

FOR THIS OUR BOUNTY by Marian F. Farrington from *THIS IS AMERICA – THE BOOK OF AMERICAN THANKSGIVING POETRY,* compiled by Gertrude Hanson, copyright 1950, used by permission of The National Thanksgiving Association; AUTUMN SNOWFALL by Earle J. Grant from *DAILY MEDITATIONS;* AUTUMN from *THE POEMS OF EMILY DICKINSON,* edited by Thomas H. Johnson, Cambridge, MA: The Belknap Press of Harvard University Press, copyright 1951, ©1955, 1979, 1983 by The President and Fellows of Harvard College; A STEP INTO THE PAST from Plimoth Plantation – The Living Museum of 17th Century Plymouth, MA; LEGACY by Vivian Reeves from *THIS IS AMERICA – THE BOOK OF AMERICAN THANKSGIVING POETRY,* compiled by Gertrude Hanson, copyright 1950, used by permission of The National Thanksgiving Association; WHEN AUTUMN SLIPS TO WINTER and FIRESIDE DREAMS from *THE LITTLE THINGS* by Garnett Ann Schultz, copyright © 1964, published by Dorrance and Company, used by permission of the author; THANKFUL from *GATES OF MEMORY* by Patience Strong, published by Frederick Muller Ltd. in 1954, used by permission of Rupert Crew, Ltd., London, England. Our sincere thanks to the following whose addresses we were unable to locate: the estate of Howard Biggar for HOME AGAIN; Margaret Bilbon for BE THANKFUL!; Elveria Blust for NATURE'S PICTURE BOOK; Mary Fink for THANKSGIVING; Inez Franck for GOODNESS AND GLORY and THANKSGIVING POSTCARDS; Lydia O. Jackson for THE BLESSINGS OF HOME; Elva Gladys Knox for PILGRIM FATHERS; Martha Corrine Love for FAMILY BLESSINGS; Gary Radcliffe for THANKSGIVING LEGACY.